THE T

A Play for Women

by

ANTHONY BOOTH

  FRENCH

LONDON
NEW YORK TORONTO SYDNEY HOLLYWOOD

© 1972 BY SAMUEL FRENCH LTD

This play is fully protected under the copyright laws of the British Commonwealth of Nations, the United States of America, and all countries of the Berne and Universal Copyright Conventions.

All rights are strictly reserved.

It is an infringement of the copyright to give any public performance or reading of this play either in its entirety or in the form of excerpts without the prior consent of the copyright owners. No part of this publication may be transmitted, stored in a retrieval system, or reproduced in any form or by any means, electronic, mechanical, photocopying, manuscript, typescript, recording, or otherwise, without the prior permission of the copyright owners.

SAMUEL FRENCH LTD, 26 SOUTHAMPTON STREET, STRAND, LONDON WC2E 7JE or their authorized agents, issue licences to amateurs to give performances of this play on payment of a fee. **The fee must be paid and the licence obtained before a performance is given.**

Licences are issued subject to the understanding that it shall be made clear in all advertising matter that the audience will witness an amateur performance; and that the names of the authors of the plays shall be included on all announcements and on all programmes.

The royalty fee indicated below is subject to contract and subject to variation at the sole discretion of Samuel French Ltd.

Basic fee for each and every
performance by amateurs   Code C
in the British Isles

In theatres or halls seating 600 or more the fee will be subject to negotiation.

In territories overseas the fee quoted above may not apply. Application must be made to our local authorized agents, or if there is no such agent, to Samuel French Ltd, London.

ISBN 0 573 13324 7

Please note our NEW ADDRESS:

**Samuel French Ltd
52 Fitzroy Street London W1P 6JR
Tel: 01 - 387 9373**

PRODUCTION NOTES

This play is already an established festival winner and meticulous care has been taken to give all movements and business to establish very clearly the mood and pace of the action.

Don't be afraid of the play, attack it, but in doing so, please take very clear note of the pauses otherwise there is a tendency to reach a climax too quickly which cannot be sustained indefinitely. The pauses are most important, not only do they steady the pace but also build tremendous suspense.

Be really tough with this girl, really pull her hair and manhandle her as she would be in real circumstances. Do not rely on tearing the shoulder of her blouse to bare the flesh as it probably won't tear. In the original production this was very carefully unpicked and lightly tacked together so that both the front and the back fell away with a sharp tug. The burning with a cigarette is simulated by reversing the cigarette at the last moment! But be sure to have a burn mark on the shoulder before the play starts. The ink used was a strong mixture of black poster paint and was most effective. It is also very effective if after the event the girl who plays Collins manages at sometime to get some on her face. There are plenty of occasions when she can do this quite naturally when she is weeping.

As regards clothing, this is straightforward. Collins wore a dark skirt and neutral blouse. Brent wore a dark skirt, white shirt with dark tie and a dark blue cardigan with pockets. Brede, who should if possible be a heavier build than the others, wore dark trousers and a windcheater. To obtain a little colour Cole wore a bright red skirt with white blouse and Adams had a simple cotton dress with a light coloured cardigan with pockets in which she kept her paper and purse.

The police car effects should be very loud.

The lighting as far as possible should be in pools covering the acting areas only. One solitary very low-wattage bulb hangs down on a wire above the table. This is the only apparent source of lighting.

The table should be old and dirty as are the chairs. The curtain on the window is almost rotting away and is suspended by an old piece of string.

The theme music for the play was "Mars" from the Planet suite.

The tabs opened in a black-out and the lights came up slowly as the music faded to reveal the room and occupants.

At the end the music started as the lights faded and the tabs fell.

ANTHONY BOOTH

CHARACTERS

Brent
  Captain in the Organization, about 45
Cole
  a witness, about 30
Adams
  the accuser, about 40
Brede
  the guard, about 45
Collins
  the accused, about 22

The action of the play takes place in the cellar of a house in a city.

The time - 3 a.m.

THE TRIAL

The room is quite stark. R, slightly angled down stage is an old kitchen table, behind which is an old chair

Below the table R is another old chair

Against the back wall, L of C, is a small window looking up to the street

Up L, a door leading to the outside

Downstage L is an old packing case about two foot six inches high on which Brent sits.

To left of the case an unconnected telephone with wires leading off L

As the CURTAIN *rises, Brent is found half sitting on the case downstage* L. *She is a dangerously quiet woman, wearing severe clothing, a jacket and a skirt which almost make up a uniform. She appears lost in thought.*

Adams, a very determined woman, stands by the window apparently waiting for someone to approach.

Cole, a sympathetic woman, younger than the other two, sits on the chair at the table. After a moment she attempts to light a cigarette but nervously drops the matches on the floor.

Cole Damn.

She retrieves the matches, lights her cigarette and puffs nervously. There is a long pause then Adams glances at her watch

Adams They are taking their time about it.
Brent They can't come direct because of the road blocks.
Adams (*irritably*) All the same . . .
Brent (*curtly*) They'll be here.

There is another long pause. Cole studies Brent, then speaks

Cole The girl they are bringing, who is she?

Brent Just a girl.
Cole (*persisting*) Yes, I know, but who?
Brent (*flatly*) It doesn't matter, we'll leave it at that.
Cole That's all very well but . . .

Brent swivels to face her

Brent (*curtly*) You are not here to ask questions.
Cole I don't even know why I am here.

Brent gets up and moves to her as she speaks

Brent As a witness.
Cole A witness to what?
Brent A trial
Cole You mean the girl?
Adams Who else?
Cole Why me?
Brent Because what you see tonight you will pass on to others and people will not be so eager to step out of line in future.

Cole stares at her intently

Cole (*slowly*) Who are you?

Brent moves to the chair below the table and half leans on the back

Brent My name is Brent. I am a captain in the Organization and am carrying out my duties as such.
Cole I see. Do I know the girl?
Brent You may do.

Cole turns to stare at Adams

Cole I know *you*, your name is Adams, isn't it?
Adams Yes.
Cole Are you in the Organization?
Adams No.
Cole Then what are you doing here?
Adams I reported the girl.
Cole I see. But I've got nothing to do with this, why have I been brought here?
Brent I told you, as a witness.
Cole I don't understand.
Brent (*curtly*) It's quite simple, it doesn't need spelling out.

She doesn't continue. Cole, suddenly frightened, bangs the table a little hysterically and rises

Cole For God's sake, tell me.

Brent spins round to face her. Cole, frightened, sits slowly and appeals to her almost in a whisper

Please.

Brent moves to behind her before speaking she then speaks evenly and factually

Brent This city is like an arsenal. We have arms, ammunition and explosives hidden in every available house, everything to destroy the occupying troops. But it isn't easy because they control the streets and have search parties and detention centres for everyone they suspect. For the first few months we were getting on top and for most people it was exciting, something to liven the boredom of their dull lives. Agreed?

Cole does not answer

Adams (*sharply*) The officer asked you a question.
Cole What?... Oh yes, I suppose, but not me, I found it horrible from the start.
Brent As time went on the novelty wore off, the disruption of normal life became irritating. Nobody likes a curfew, no-one likes being searched in the street and people don't really enjoy the sight of blood. So, what had once been a scythe, turned into a two-edged sword and started to cut the handlers.

Cole What do you mean?
Brent (*moves to above table*) I mean that the people sickened of the long drawn-out struggle.

She walks slowly down to the box almost speaking to herself, staring straight ahead

They could no longer see that what to us was a sign of strength in the blowing up of a pub in the heart of the army territory, to them meant losing some of their lives and the destruction of their property, so they took, or rather are taking the cowards way out. They secretly inform the army where they can find hidden arms, where there is likely to be a raid and when there is going to be a break out of one of the detention centres.

She sits on the case and faces the girl

So . . . the people must be reminded.

Cole You are going to make an example of this girl?

Brent Yes.

Cole (*quietly*) You are going to . . . to execute her?

Brent If the case is proved, but more than likely on this occasion we will make an example of her for people to see, so that the lesson goes home. She will be the first courier as it were.

Cole And my part in this?

Brent Just a spectator, but afterwards you will talk, you will tell people what you saw and perhaps they will think twice before indulging in further sabotage of our efforts to free the country. No-one likes to think it might happen to them.

A police car goes by, its siren blaring. Brent speaks sharply to Adams

Pull that curtain!

Adams does so. The car carries on swiftly down the road

Have I made myself clear?

Cole (*quietly*) Yes.

There is quite a pause

Adams They should be here by now. Do you suppose anything has happened?

Brent There is always the chance.

Adams How long do we wait?

Brent gets up glancing at her watch

Brent There is no time limit.

Adams Yes, but . . .

Brent moves to her irritably, she speaks sharply

Brent You were the one who put this girl up to us, she was your selection and you are the chief witness.

Adams So?

Brent (*curtly*) So you sweat it out like everyone else.

There is a pause. Brent returns to the case and sits. Cole stares at Adams

Cole (*quietly*) You reported this girl?
Adams Yes.
Cole (*softly*) How could you?
Adams (*turning to her*) I would have been a traitor if I hadn't.
Cole I wouldn't have called it that.
Adams Do you know of people who have given information to the military?
Cole I don't know them, but I've heard a few names.
Adams And you have done nothing about it?
Cole No.
Adams (*shortly*) Then you are no better than she is.
Brent (*drily*) Possibly, but then she is not on trial here.
Adams (*angrily*) I don't agree, the principle is the same. If she knew that someone . . .

There is a solitary knock at the door. A momentary pause

Brent They are here. Let them in.

Adams starts to move to the door L but pauses as Brent speaks again

I only want the girl and Brede in here, tell the others to wait outside until we have finished.

Adams goes out L. Cole rises nervously

You had better stand by that chair below the table and you will be well advised not to interrupt.

Cole moves below the table, staring nervously at the door. After a moment Adams returns and moves to above the table

Adams (*curtly*) In here.

Brede, a strong woman of about fifty, wearing trousers and a heavy pullover, enters. She thrusts Collins, a very frightened girl of about twenty, ahead of her, holding her arm tightly. The girl is blindfolded and has plaster across her mouth to prevent her screaming

Cole (*quietly*) Oh God!
Brent Quiet. Take the blindfold and plaster off.

Brede does so and the girl, dazed, looks round the room terrified

Sit her in the chair.

Brede pushes the girl roughly towards the chair behind the table

Brede (*harshly*) Sit.

She thrusts the girl heavily in the chair. The girl suddenly breaks. She places her head in her arms on the table and weeps copiously. They watch her quite unmoved. Cole takes a hesitant step towards her

Brent (*curtly*) Stay where you are. (*To Brede.*) Give her some water.

Brede pours half a glass of water from the carafe on the table, lifts the girl's head and gives her the glass

Brede Drink this, you'll feel better.

The girl takes it, almost choking over her first gulp, she stares around her terrified as she sips. Brede finally takes the glass from her, then takes up her position behind her. Collins stares at Brent

Collins (*whispering*) Who . . . who are you?
Brent I'm an officer in the Organization.
Collins Where am I?
Brent The other side of the city.
Collins Why have I been brought here?
Brent To answer some questions.
Collins About what?
Brent We'll come to that.
Collins Why blindfold and gag me?
Brent To prevent you from screaming and also knowing where you were being taken.
Collins Yes, but . . .
Brent (*curtly*) Before you continue, have you been roughly treated on your way here?

The girl does not answer

Adams (*harshly from the window*) Answer the officer.

The girl looks up and recognizes Adams. She half rises but Brede pushes her back

The Trial

Coilins You!
Brede Sit.
Collins What are you doing here?
Adams (*shortly*) You'll see.
Brent You haven't answered my question yet.
Collins (*bewildered*) Question?
Brent Were you roughly treated?
Collins (*quietly*) No. . . . No, not really, except they held me while they put the plaster on my face.
Brent (*half smiling*) Well, that is understandable, isn't it?
Collins (*quietly*) I suppose. (*She pauses for a moment then speaks wildly*) What is happening to my mother and father?
Brent Nothing, they are at home waiting for your return.
Collins How can you say things like that?
Brent (*severely*) When the women collected you from your house, did they molest your parents in any way?
Collins (*dazed*) No.
Brent Exactly, we have no quarrel with them, only sympathy.
Collins Sympathy?
Adams That their daughter is a traitor.
Collins (*wildly*) Me! I don't understand.
Adams (*shortly*) You soon will.

Brent moves to the table

Brent What is your name?
Collins. Anne Marie.
Brent Anne Marie, what?
Collins Collins.
Brent Tell me about yourself.
Collins Tell you what?
Brent What do you do?
Collins I'm a school teacher.
Brent Family?
Collins You know that already, I have a mother and father.
Brent No brothers or sisters?

The girl shakes her head

  Are you engaged?
Collins (*quickly*) No.
Brent Boy friend?

Collins (*hesitating*) No.

Adams moves quickly to the top of the table, she shouts at Collins

Adams (*hotly*) She's lying.
Collins (*desperately*) I haven't, I tell you. . . . I haven't.
Brent Adams seems to disagree with you.
Collins (*vehemently*) What has she got to do with it?
Brent She is responsible for your being here tonight. We'll start again. Have you a boy friend?
Collins (*shouting*) No.
Adams (*shouting*) You lying little bitch, everyone knows you spend every minute of your spare time with that army sergeant.
Collins (*wildly, in tears*) It's not true.
Adams Course it is, his name is Fenner, John Fenner.
Collins (*beating the table wildly*) No, no, no.
Adams (*to Cole*) You've seen them together, haven't you?
Cole I . . . no.
Adams Then you must be the only person in the neighbourhood who hasn't.
Cole (*angrily*) I tell you I haven't. Why don't you believe the girl?
Adams Keep out of this, it's none of your business.
Cole (*furious*) It is my business to stand by someone being treated like this.
Adams (*angrily*) And I say . . .
Brent (*curtly*) You've had your say.

Adams faces her angrily and for a moment there is a silent clash of personalities. Adams finally shrugs her shoulders and returns to the window. Brent turns back to the girl, speaking evenly

This army sergeant.
Collins (*wildly*) I keep telling you . . .
Brent (*persisting*) This army sergeant, what unit is he in?

Collins hangs her head in silent defiance. Brent, taking her time, half sits on the front of the table and pours herself a glass of water. She goes on evenly

I don't think you realize the position you are in. We can, if necessary, be tough. Answer the questions truthfully and you will save yourself a lot of grief. (*She takes a sip of water*) Do you know Sergeant Fenner?

Collins (*whispering*) Yes.
Brent What is your relationship with him?
Cole (*angrily*) You've no right . . .
Brent (*very sharply*) I've every right. (*To Collins, evenly*) Is he just a friend . . . your lover perhaps?
Collins (*angrily*) He is not.

From now on the interrogation builds up in speed and pressure

Brent What is the position, then?
Collins We—we are engaged.
Brent You don't wear a ring.

Collins covers her hand, guiltily, turning away

Collins We . . . we don't want anyone to know.
Brent Obviously. What about your parents, do they approve?
Collins They don't know.
Brent Do they know him?
Collins No, we have to meet secretly.

Brent gets up, glass in hand

Brent I see. What is his unit?
Collins (*defiantly*) Find out.
Brent (*harshly*) Is it true he belongs to the S.I.B.?
Collins What's that?
Brent Special Investigation Branch, Intelligence. Well?

Collins stares at her defiantly. Suddenly Brent throws the contents of her glass of water in the girl's face, viciously

(*Shouting*) Answer me.

Collins gives a little cry at the shock then buries her head in her arms on the table, sobbing bitterly. Cole takes a step towards her

Cole (*passionately*) For God's sake, she's had enough.
Brent (*very harshly*) We've only just started.

She nods to Brede who grabs the girl by her hair and pulls her head back viciously. Collins screams

Brede (*harshly*) Answer the questions.
Brent (*loud*) Is he a member of the S.I.B.?
Collins (*sobbing*) I don't know, he didn't tell me.

Brent And you never asked him what he did?
Collins No, he just said he had an office job at headquarters, that's all I know, I swear it.
Adams (*shouting*) She's lying.
Collins I am not.

Brent nods to Brede who releases the girl. She sobs bitterly, her head in her arms on the table. Brent walks slowly to above the left end of the table. She surveys the weeping girl for a few seconds before carrying on

Brent (*quietly and evenly*) Where do you meet?
Collins In a cellar club downtown—sometimes we go for a walk on the heath.
Brent He's taking a risk, isn't he?

Collins stops sobbing, she answers the questions fearfully

Collins He always changes into civilian clothes.
Brent (*half smiles*) Wise man. What do you talk about?
Collins (*whispering*) Things—just things.
Brent (*sharply*) Speak up.
Collins Private things . . . like our future when all this is over.
Brent You mean your marriage?
Collins (*whispering*) Yes.
Adams How can you marry one of them? You've seen what they do to innocent civilians.
Cole (*riled*) What about the civilians who snipe at them, who throw bombs then hide behind crowds of women.
Adams (*angrily*) Are you defending them?
Cole (*topping her*) No, but there is the other side, too. They never asked to be brought here, this isn't their quarrel.
Adams (*shouting*) You had better watch your tongue, it can bring you a lot of trouble. . . .
Cole (*furious*) I'll say what I damn well please. . . .

Collins turns to her agonized

Collins Please don't . . . thank you, but she's right, it could do you a lot of harm.

Cole and Adams face each other for a moment in silent anger then Adams with a slight smile turns back to the window again.

The Trial

In the silence that follows Brede lights a cigarette. Brent, after a moment, wanders down C

Brent (*evenly*) What are your personal feelings about our struggle?
Collins (*helplessly*) I haven't any, all I want is for it to end. . . . I never wanted to be mixed up in it . . . *all* I want to do is to teach.
Brent (*quietly*) Very commendable.

The pressure builds up again, Brent is relentless in her cross-examination

(*Curtly*) What do you and your sergeant talk about?
Collins (*a little desperately*) I've told you already . . . personal things.
Brent (*quickly*) And nothing else?
Collins No.
Brent (*searchingly*) How many houses near you have arms hidden in them?
Collins (*in tears*) I don't know.
Brent (*persisting*) About how many in your *street*, for instance.
Collins (*shouting*) I don't know, I don't know.

Collins stands defiantly. Brede takes her by the shoulder and sits her down, viciously ripping the girl's dress as she does so, exposing her bare shoulder. Collins screams, putting her face in her hands and sobbing

Cole (*angrily*) Is it necessary to be quite so brutal?
Brent (*shouting her down*) Don't interrupt.

She goes to the table quickly and bangs her hands hard on it, she shouts at the girl

Think again, do you know of any houses where these things are stored?
Collins (*hysterically*) No, no, I don't.
Adams (*shouting*) Don't lie!
Collins (*desperately*) I'm not, I don't know any. None.

Brent straightens up

Brent (*quietly*) We can make you talk, you know.
Collins (*defiantly through her tears*) Try, just try,

Brent stares at her for a moment then takes a step back and nods to Brede. Brede blows the ash off her cigarette, then stubs it out viciously on the girl's bare shoulder. Collins screams with the shock and pain

Cole (*pleading*) Oh God, leave her alone, for God's sake leave her alone.

A police car approaches, its siren blaring. Collins jumps to her feet and tries to run to the window

Collins (*screaming*) Help me, help me . . . for God's sake help me. . . .

Brede flings herself on the girl putting her hand over her mouth to stop her screaming. The car passes unheeding. Brede throws the girl back into the chair again where she buries her head in her arms on the table and sobs loud and hysterically. Brent surveys her for quite a long time then moves to the table waiting for the sobbing to subside a little before she speaks. She leans on the table

Brent (*quietly*) How many houses, Collins, how many?
Collins (*sobbing*) Four . . . no, five I think.
Brent (*straightening up*) That's better.
Brede (*quietly*) Do you want some water?

The girl shakes her head, still sobbing

Brent Connect the phone.
Brede Right.

Brede crosses to left of the packing case and starts to connect the phone to the wires leading off stage. She is quick and efficient and the job takes about half a minute. Brent wanders to the box, glancing at a piece of paper she takes from her pocket. The silence is broken by the continuous quiet sobbing of Collins. The wires connected, Brede tests the phone by listening, then places it on the upstage end of the case

It's working.

Brent nods then Brede takes up her position behind the girl again

Brent (*quietly*) Is there anything else you want to tell me?

Collins shakes her head. Brent nods to Adams then sits on the case

She's all yours, Adams.

Adams comes down to the front of the table

Adams Right, Collins, we'll talk about these houses.
Collins (*helplessly*) No, no, I've told you all I know.
Adams You've told us nothing.
Collins It's no good, I can't, I just can't.
Adams Think again, there is plenty of time. (*There is no reaction*) All right, here are a few reminders. (*She takes out a small piece of paper from her pocket and puts it on the table*) On May the eighth you brought back a case from school to your home. . . . Well, didn't you?
Collins (*dully*) Yes.
Adams It contained ten pounds of gelignite.
Collins (*quickly*) I didn't know.
Adams (*harshly*) You must have known, ten pounds is a lot of weight to carry nearly half a mile.
Collins I tell you, I didn't know.
Adams Didn't you open it when you got back?
Collins. No, it was locked.
Adams Weren't you curious?
Collins Yes.
Adams What did you think it was?
Collins (*wearily*) I don't know, ammunition perhaps.
Adams But even suspecting that, you took it just the same?
Collins Yes.
Adams (*sarcastically*) You don't add up, do you? Just now you said you didn't want to be mixed up in anything. If that's true, why didn't you refuse to take the case?
Collins (*with spirit*) Because the two men who gave it to me threatened to hurt my parents if I didn't.
Adams And you believed them?
Cole (*angrily*) And why not, the house three doors away from me was blown up because the people wouldn't co-operate.
Adams And who do you suppose blew it up?
Cole You know damn well. . . . *Them.*
Adams Do *you* co-operate?
Cole They haven't asked me.
Adams But if they did?
Cole I'd be a fool not to.

Adams stares at her a moment then turns her attention to the girl again

Adams To get back to the case. What did you do with it?
Collins I took it to a house.
Adams Let's be more specific, which house?
Collins (*dully*) Number thirty-one Tondin Street.
Adams Number thirty-one. What did you do after that?
Collins I—I can't remember.
Brent Think, it's important.
Collins (*a little desperately*) I tell you, I can't remember.
Adams You met your friend in the Cellar Club.
Collins (*dully*) I may have.
Adams There is no may about it. You did.
Collins If you say so.
Adams You got back at eleven o'clock.
Collins (*with spirit*) I can't, the curfew starts at nine.
Adams (*forcefully*) He brought you back in an army patrol wagon and dropped you behind your house.

The girl hangs her head, silent

Well, didn't he?
Collins (*whispering*) Yes.
Adams That's better.
Brent The Cellar Club closes at a quarter to nine, where did you go until eleven?
Collins (*dully*) On the heath, I think.
Brent Let's be more accurate.
Collins I told you, on the heath.
Brent But if it was after curfew, you would have been spotted.
Collins We went by car.
Brent Civilian or army?
Cole It must have been army, no civilian cars are allowed on the streets after curfew.

Brent is annoyed at the interruption, she stands

Brent (*viciously*) I'm warning you for the last time. Keep out of this (*To Collins*) Well?
Collins It was an army truck.

Brent moves a little towards her

Brent And you went on the heath?
Collins Yes.

Adams moves angrily to above the left end of the table, shouting

Adams You bloody little liar!

She comes down to the end of the table and bangs it with her hands

You never went on the heath. I'll tell you where you spent two hours . . . at S.I.B. headquarters.
Collins (*vehemently*) I didn't, I swear it, I didn't. . . . I've never been there, never.
Adams (*screaming*) Liar!

The girl beats the table with her fists, hysterically

Collins (*shouting*) No, no, no, no.

She weeps for a moment, then after a few seconds she pulls herself together a little

What is all this leading up to?
Adams It's quite simple really. No-one with the exception of the area commander, the occupants of thirty-one Tondin Street and yourself, knew there was anything hidden in that house.
Collins What has this got to do with me?
Brent The Commander and the occupants are not likely to give information to anyone, are they?
Collins No.
Brent (*quietly*) Which leaves you.
Collins I wouldn't say anything.
Brent Wouldn't or didn't.
Collins What do you mean?
Brent The house was raided at two o'clock the same night, all the stuff hidden was lost and the occupants were sent to a detention camp.

The girl stares at her for a few moments

Collins And you think I told them?
Adams Who else could it have been?
Collins (*vehemently*) But I didn't, I swear it.
Adams You say you spent the night on the heath?
Collins Yes.

Adams (*shouting*) You are lying!
Collins I'm not.
Adams Yes, you are. No-one was allowed on the heath, it was the night of the break-out from Darren Detention Centre, the whole countryside was swarming with police and troops.

There is a long pause

Brent (*quietly*) Didn't you see them . . . or were you otherwise engaged?

The girl does not reply. Brent speaks sharply

Where were you? Let's have the truth this time.

The girl hangs her head shamefully and half turns away

Collins (*quietly*) I've a friend on the Gordin Estate . . . she lets us have a room.
Adams (*loudly*) You dirty little slut . . . you filthy little . . .
Brent (*firmly*) All right, that's enough, Adams.
Adams But with one of their soldiers . . .
Brent She is not being tried on moral grounds.
Adams I say it's a crime to associate with them in any way.
Brent I agree, but in a different category.

Adams faces Brent in silent fury. She would like to pusue the argument but realizes that Brent will not continue it. With an angry gesture she returns to the window. Brent turns back to the girl again

And you swear you never mentioned anything to your sergeant?
Collins I told him nothing.

Brent eyes her for a moment then walks slowly to the right end of the table. She comes face to face with Cole. Cole stares at her for a moment in quiet defiance then moves away to the chair on her left. Brent pauses just to the right of the girl

Brent (*gently*) Do you intend to marry him?
Collins (*whispering*) Yes.
Brent I see. If your relationship is that close, you obviously have no secrets.
Collins No, I know all about him and he knows all about me.
Brent And I suspect us as well.

Collins (*quickly*) No, I never discuss anything like that with him. He wouldn't ask me anyway.

Brent moves to behind her, speaking quite evenly

Brent But if, as you say, you don't want this struggle to go on any longer, wouldn't it be natural to give him information which would enable the army to clean up the area much quicker
Collins (*dully*) I suppose.

Brent moves to above the left end of the table

Brent I mean, you wouldn't be the only one, we have several informers on our list.
Collins (*vehemently*) How can I make you understand, I am not an informer.
Brent You know what happens to informers, don't you?
Collins (*whispering*) I've heard.
Brent They are shot.
Cole (*sharply*) That's murder.
Brent You think so? You execute a spy in war, we are at war, it is as simple as that.

Brent moves to the front of the table

We have a punishment for fraternization as well. Give me your hand.

The girl shrinks back in terror

Collins (*terrified*) No . . . no.
Brent I am not going to hurt you.
Collins No.

Brent nods to Brede who seizes the girl's hand and forces it palm upwards on to the table. Brent takes a small phial from her pocket and pours the contents onto the girl's hand. She screams involuntarily and drags her hand away and stares at it, covered in ink, in horror

Brent That is a small sample. It's printer's ink, quite harmless but difficult to remove. (*She moves to the box, speaking as she goes and picks up an old rag from the top of it*) We also cut the offender's hair off, then pour two gallons of this over them, they usually co-operate after that. Do I make myself clear?

Collins (*whispering*) Yes.

Brent Good. (*She moves to the table and throws the rag on top of it*) Here, clean yourself up with this. (*She returns to the box and sits, the girl tries to clean her hand*) Right, Adams, carry on.

Adams comes down to the front of the desk

Adams Right, we'll have a few more facts.

Collins (*helplessly*) No, I can't answer any more questions, please. . . . Please let me go.

Adams (*relentlessly*) On the night of May the twenty-second, you helped carry stolen uniforms and rifles into a house in Doncaster Street.

Collins I—I may have.

Adams You know damn well you did, I was with you, there were six of us altogether.

Collins (*wearily*) Perhaps.

Brede (*sharply*) Answer her.

Collins Yes, yes, I did.

Adams Two days later the house was raided.

Collins What are you implying?

Adams It seems a strange coincidence.

Cole (*aggressively*) Why should it be? It could have been any of the four other people.

Adams It could be, but I very much doubt it. It is more likely that Collins met her sergeant the next day and quietly passed on the information.

Cole That's what you *want* to believe, isn't it?

Adams That's what I do believe.

Collins (*quickly*) I couldn't have anyway.

Adams Why not?

Collins I was so upset over the whole business that I was ill in bed for three days afterwards.

Adams That's a convenient story.

Cole Which means that she was still in bed a whole day *after* the raid.

Adams (*angrily*) She's lying, can't you see, she's lying.

Collins (*vehemently*) It's true, I swear it. Ask my parents. You can check with the school, I had to have a doctor's certificate to give them in any case. (*Brokenly to Brent*) It's simple enough to check.

The Trial

Brent (*quietly*) Don't worry, we will.
Adams On June the third . . .

The girl starts to break down again

Collins No, no, no, I can't go on, I just can't.
Adams On June the third, we received a consignment of rifles and gelignite which were hidden in a house five doors from where you live.
Collins I didn't have anything to do with it.
Adams Not the actual handling, no. You made such a fuss that we decided to use you as a look-out on the street corner. You remember that, don't you?
Collins Yes.
Adams Just as we had finished you were approached by a patrol, that's true, isn't it?
Collins Yes.
Adams And you went off with them. What did you tell them?
Collins I told you the next day.
Adams Tell us again, the officer would like to hear it.

The girl falters, she appeals to Brent quietly

Collins Could I have some water, please?

Brent nods and Brede pours some into a glass and gives it to the girl. She sips it gratefully. There is quite a pause

Adams Tell the officer.
Collins The sergeant in charge of the patrol asked me what I was doing on the street after curfew.
Adams What did you tell him?
Collins I told him I was looking for my cat.
Adams You said it was your dog last time.
Collins I couldn't have, we haven't got a dog.
Brent Go on.
Collins He wasn't satisfied so they took me back to section headquarters for further questioning.
Brent Yes?
Collins The officer asked me the usual things like, where did I live, who could identify me and so on, and in the middle of it a sergeant came in, he was a friend of my fiancé. He obviously

recognized me and spoke to the officer quietly for a few moments. I suppose he vouched for me.

Brent What happened after that?

Collins Nothing. They gave me a cup of tea and dropped me off at my house in the patrol vehicle.

Adams You seem to make a habit of being taken home in army transport.

Brent And you told them nothing?

Collins I swear it.

Brent Did you know that the house was raided five days later?

The girl lowers her head and nods

Brede (*sharply*) Answer the officer.

Collins (*whispering*) Yes, yes, I did hear.

Adams Quite a remarkable coincidence, wouldn't you say?

Cole Do you really believe she informed?

Adams Yes, I do.

Cole Then you must be naïve.

Adams What do you mean?

Cole Knowing how quickly this stuff is needed and moved around, do you honestly believe they would wait five whole days before raiding the place?

Adams is taken aback

Adams (*blustering*) Well . . . er . . . well . . .

Cole (*sharply*) Well, come on.

Adams appeals to Brent

Adams (*angrily*) Are you going to allow her to cross-examine me?

Brent (*evenly*) It appears she has a valid point. Answer her question. Do you think they would wait that long?

Adams (*defiantly*) They might.

Cole Why?

Adams If this girl is an informant they might do it to cover up for her. If they had raided the house the same night or the next day, it would have been obvious where the information came from.

Cole (*slowly*) And you honestly believe that?

Adams It's possible.

Cole But not probable. (*To Brent*) What is your opinion?

The Trial

Brent I am not here to give opinions, merely to listen to evidence.
Cole Yes, but surely . . .
Brede (*harshly*) You heard what the officer said.

Cole subsides, turning away in frustration

Brent (*she stands*) You were in a position to give information. As a point of interest, why didn't you?
Collins Because—well, I suppose I want to remain neutral.
Brent There are no neutrals, only cowards.
Collins (*quietly*) Well I'm a coward then.
Adams (*harshly*) Self-confessed.

There is a pause

Brent Have you any other evidence?
Adams Yes, the most important piece.
Brent Continue.

Brent sits on the box again. Adams moves to above the left end of the table, leaning towards the girl

Adams Last Friday, my husband carried out a gelignite raid on the Mannering quarry. You know that because I asked you if you could keep watch from your bedroom window and flash a torch if any of the patrols came down the street. That's true, isn't it?
Collins Yes.
Adams My husband managed to get it into our house unseen. You were the only other person who knew where it was hidden.
Cole The others on the raid must have known.
Adams No, he told no-one where he was going to hide it. It could have been any of a dozen houses.
Brent Get to the point.
Adams You met your sergeant after school the next day, didn't you?
Collins Yes, it was my birthday, he was off duty and took me out to supper, but I was home by the curfew.
Adams Very convenient. By another of those strange coincidences, the army raided our house that night, recovered all the explosive and arrested my husband. He is in a camp now awaiting trial.
Brent What have you got to say to that?

Collins What can I say? I did keep watch because she insisted that our house was the best place and I did meet my fiancé the next day, but I never discussed anything with him about the emergency, I never do, it's a sort of agreement we have.

Adams (*shouting*) Lies, all lies. Thanks to you I've lost my husband, don't you realize what that means, I've lost my husband.

Cole Where were you at the time?

Adams Where? Staying the night with a friend. (*To Collins*) He was a good man and didn't want me to take any risk and this is how he was repaid, by one of his own people.

Cole (*furiously*) You hypocrite, you bloody hypocrite. You hated his guts, everyone knows that you have been carrying on with Frank Owens from the Park Estate for months now and you have the gall to stand there, broken-hearted about a man you would have left years ago if you had had the chance.

Adams comes down in front of the table, furious. Cole moves in towards her and they meet face to face, c

Adams (*shouting*) My private life has nothing to do with this.

Cole (*angrily*) But it has. You seem to forget that you were the only other person who knew your husband was using your home that night to store explosives.

Adams What are you implying?

Cole (*very forcefully*) Simple. That it would have been all too easy to phone the army anonymously and tell them. You weren't there to be caught, so you weren't involved. Your husband very conveniently taken off your hands for good and there was someone else handy to take the blame.

Adams (*screaming*) You bitch, you bloody bitch.

Adams suddenly loses control and seizes Cole by the hair and they fight wildly, rolling on the floor and screaming abuse at each other. They fight viciously for a few moments then Brent, quite unmoved nods to Brede who wades in and separates them. She thrusts Adams harshly to the centre and half kneels between her and Cole to keep them apart. Adams raises her body a little from the floor with her hands and glares at Cole. She speaks gaspingly

I'll get you, so help me God, I'll get you if it's the last thing I do.

Brent stands. She surveys Adams with distaste

The Trial

Brent Pull yourself together, Adams, this is a trial, not a public brawl.

Adams turns her head as if to answer her back

Wait by the window.

Adams glares at her defiantly for a moment then gets to her feet slowly and moves to the window. Brent turns to Cole

Are you all right?
Cole Yes—yes, I'm all right.

Brede helps Cole to her feet and she slumps in the chair R. Brent sits again and Brede returns to behind the girl

Brent (*quietly*) Come here, Collins. Come here.
Collins is terrified, she is unwilling to move but Brede half lifts her out of the chair, takes her round the top end of the table and thrusts her down towards Brent

You've heard all the accusations?
Collins (*whispering*) Yes.
Brent Have you anything to add to what you have already stated?
Collins (*imploring*) No, only to repeat that I have never at any time given information to the army.

Brent surveys her for a moment then takes a small card from her pocket

Brent Well, here is your chance to make amends.

Bent hands the card to the girl who reads it

Collins What . . . what is this?
Brent I am going to dial the S.I.B. When they answer you will read out to them what is on that card, nothing else, no name, nothing. You understand?
Collins I can't—I can't.
Brent Why not, it's quite simple.
Collins (*brokenly*) You are forcing me to inform and when I've done it you have got your evidence and I won't do it.
Brent (*firmly*) You will.
Collins No, never—never.

Brent nods to Brede who takes the girl's arm and twists it viciously behind her back. The girl screams with pain

Collins Oh, God, you are breaking my arm.
Brent (*grimly*) You will read the message.
Collins (*shouting*) No, no.

Brede twists her arm a little further then throws her down at Brent's feet where she sobs uncontrollably. Brent stands

Brent You will not be held responsible. No-one outside this room will ever know.
Collins How can I be sure?
Brent You have my word.
Collins How do I know you won't break it?
Brent You don't. Very well, I'll put it another way. Unless you make this call, your Sergeant Fenner will be put on our list for personal execution.

The girl looks up at her, her hands clasped, almost begging. She speaks with difficulty through her tears

Collins You can't—you can't do that.
Brent You believe *that*, don't you?

The girl lowers her head, beaten

Collins Yes . . . oh yes.

Brent moves to above the case and picks up the phone

Brent You will say nothing more than what is written on that card. (*She dials four numbers, then after a moment speaks into the phone*) S.I.B. Headquarters? Hold the line, I have a call for you.

Brent holds out the phone to the girl who takes it. She looks up at Brent hoping for a reprieve but there is no reaction. Speaking with difficulty through her sobs, she reads slowly from the card

Collins Here is some information for you. . . . There are six machine-guns, ten rifles and two thousand rounds of ammunition at fifty-six Dale Road . . . they are hidden . . . they are hidden under the floorboards of the back bedroom . . . it is due out tomorrow night.

Collins stops and looks at Brent. The operator is heard faintly

Operator Who is calling, please? Please answer. Who is calling?

Brent cuts off the call very quickly and takes the phone from the girl, replacing it on the cradle

Collins (*brokenly*) What have I done . . . what have I done?

Adams (*smugly*) Something worthwhile for a change. There is a hundred pounds of gelignite in that house, it is one big booby trap. The moment they force the bedroom door it will go sky high taking with it some of your precious friends.

The girl buries her head in her hands and sobs bitterly

Collins Oh, no—no, no, no.

Brent lets her sob for a moment before speaking

Brent You may go.

The girl looks up at her in disbelief. Brent speaks gently

   I said, you may go.
Collins You don't believe I informed against anyone?
Brent (*slowly*) No.
Collins Oh, bless you—bless you.

Impulsively Collins takes Brent's hand and kisses it. Brent, slightly embarrassed half turns away from her

Brent (*curtly*) Get her out of here.

Brede helps the girl to her feet

Brede Come on.
Brent When you have handed her over come back here.
Brede Right.

Half supporting the girl she takes her out of the door up L. *Brent moves up and stares at the door. Suddenly there is a terrifying scream which is quickly muffled and replaced by groans which fade Cole moves in a little*

Cole (*brokenly*) You said you believed her.
Brent I know.
Cole It was a trick.

Brent There is no trick, she has been cleared of the charge.
Cole Then what's happening to her now?

Brent moves down to left of the case

Brent She is paying the penalty for fraternization.
Cole What will they do?
Brent Shave her head, douse her with ink and tie her to a lamp-post near a busy bus stop.
Cole For how long?
Brent Until the police or army free her. No civilian will dare touch her.

Brede enters and comes C

Brede They have taken her away.

Adams moves down a little to face Brent

Adams (*harshly*) I can't understand why you let her go.
Brent Because I believed her.

Adams moves in a little angrily

Adams And you took her word against mine?
Brent Yes.
Adams But it *must* have been her, she was the common factor on every occasion.
Brent (*firmly*) And so were you.
Adams What do you mean?

Brent moves up stage as she speaks

Brent You used this girl to cover up your own activity.
Adams What makes you say that?
Brent Because too many things remain unexplained.
Adams Such as?

Brent moves down to her a little

Brent We'll come to that. Tell me something, is it true what this woman said about you and your husband being on bad terms?
Adams (*shrugs*) We have our differences.
Cole Differences! You've always said you hated his guts, everyone knows.

Adams moves to her angrily

Adams All right then, I hate his guts, there is no crime in that is there?
Brent How long have you been associating with this other man?
Adams What's that got to do with it?
Brent (*curtly*) How long?
Adams (*surly*) About a year.
Brent Are you having an affair with him?

Adams half sits on the table

Adams Well, we don't sit around and play happy families if that's what you mean.
Brent Does your husband give you any money?
Adams Him! You have to be joking.
Brent moves down to her
Brent But you have got money?
Adams (*shrugs*) Just a few pounds.
Brent What do you call a few?
Adams Twenty-five—thirty maybe.

There is a pause

Brent Your arithmetic is a little out. Right now you have seven hundred and fifty-nine pounds to your credit.

Adams stands quickly

Adams How do you know that?
Brent We have access to information everywhere. Where did it come from?
Adams From—from my friend.
Brent Your friend has been out of work for eleven months, he has been living on assistance.
Adams (*defiantly*) I can't see what this has got to . . .
Brent (*curtly*) Give me your purse.
Adams I will not.
Brent (*sharply*) Get it from her.

Brent steps away down L and Brede moves in and after a tussle takes the small purse from Adam's jacket pocket which she hands to Brent, holding Adams back who is protesting wildly

Adams (*shouting*) You've no right.

Brent (*curtly*) I've every right. (*She opens it and takes out two five-pound notes. She takes a small piece of paper from her pocket and compares the numbers on it with those on the notes*) The numbers on these notes are identical with the ones issued by the bank to the paymaster at S.I.B. Headquarters.

Adams (*protesting wildly*) That doesn't prove anything, I could have got those from a shop.

Brent moves to her angrily

Brent As change from what? (*She pauses*) The notes you pay into your post office account from time to time are also accounted as coming from the S.I.B. We have all the numbers and in your case they always run consectively. Do you want any further proof?

Adams stares at her, she seems dazed at the sudden change of events. She attempts to speak

Adams I—I . . .
Brent Yes?

Adams lowers her head, she is beaten

You made two bad mistakes tonight. In your eagerness to cover yourself by blaming the girl, you said that no-one but the occupants of the house and the area Commander knew about the gelignite she took to Tondin Street. *You* did, however, this was a close secret but *you* knew . . . secondly, no-one other than my immediate superior and myself knew the contents of the phone message the girl made tonight . . . but you did, you knew about the booby trap and you couldn't resist telling her. For a long time now we have known there has been a security leak and tonight you played right into our hands.

She moves to the phone and starts dialling. Adams falls to her knees sobbing, begging for mercy

Adams (*sobbing*) I'll pay back all the money, I swear it. . . . Oh, God, don't take it any further, I didn't realize . . .

Brent is connected to her number

Brent (*into phone*) You needn't look any further, we've got her. (*She puts the phone down and moves to Adams. She looks down* *on her with scorn*) You will be shot, Adams, without compunction or regret. (*Angrily she flings the purse across the back of the weeping woman*)

The theme music starts, the lights fade

CURTAIN

FURNITURE AND PROPERTY LIST

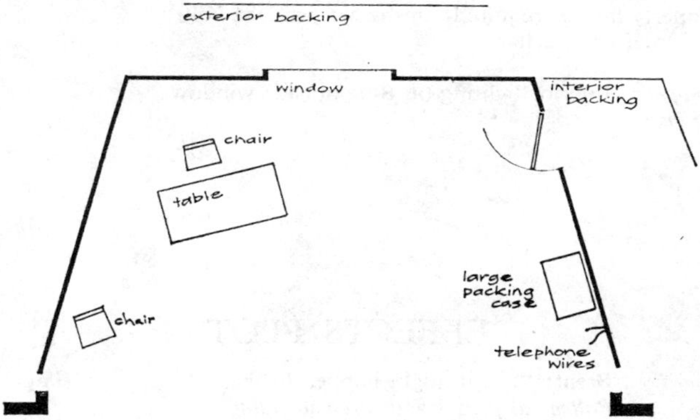
exterior backing
window
interior
backing
chair
table
large
packing
case
chair
telephone
wires

On stage: Kitchen table. *On it:* bottle of water and glasses
Kitchen chair
1 packing case. *On it:* rag
In wall down stage: telephone wires leading off stage

On floor: Bag containing telephone and connecting wires
Window curtain

Personal: **Cole:** cigarettes, matches
Adams: wristwatch, purse with two £5 notes
Brent: phial of dark liquid, card, piece of paper

LIGHTING PLOT

Property fittings required: unshaded pendant bulb
    Interior: a cellar

To open: Interior lighting on Blue outside window
No cues

EFFECTS PLOT

Cue 1	**Brent:** ". . . it might happen to them." *Police car passes with siren sounding*	(Page 4)
Cue 2	**Cole:** ". . . leave her alone." *Police car passes with siren sounding*	(Page 12)